The Way Home

The Way Home

poems by
Len Anderson

Hummingbird Press
Santa Cruz, California

Acknowledgement is gratefully made to the following publications, in which
many of these poems first appeared:

Caesura: "Into Being"

Catamaran Literary Reader: "The Way Home"

DNA: "Family," "A Simple Bow"

Hilltromper: "Conversation," "The Trees"

Phren-Z: "The Day," "The Forest," "Cave Art," "The Fashioning of Wings,"
"In My 395th Lifetime," "Yet Another Revelation" (as "Revelation No. 403")

Rattle: "The Basic Question"

Red Wheelbarrow: "Twenty Aphorisms," "Solid Ground," "The Haunting,"
"Search Party for God," "Growing Up," "Duty," "Drop"

The Sand Hill Review: "Who Is That Singing?" "Just Another Dharma," "Blossom"

Miramar: "The Empty Church"

Cover art by T. Mike Walker
Author and cover art photos by Don Monkerud
Book design by Kathleen Roberts

Hummingbird Press
P.O. Box 32
Soquel, CA 95073
https://dasulliv1.wixsite.com/hummingbirdpress
Printed by Bookmobile

Acknowledgements

The author and thus this collection of poems have been nourished by the love and support of Elke Maus. These poems owe much to the fellowship, encouragement, inspiration and critique of many dear poetry friends, including:

Emerald Street Poets: Marcia Adams, Virgil Banks, Julia Alter-Canvin, Dane Cervine, Jenny D'Angelo, Kathleen Flowers, Ted Kagy, Robin Lysne, Joanna Martin, Phyllis Mayfield, Adela Najarro, Maggie Paul, Stuart Presley, Carol Rodriguez, Joan Safajek, Lisa Simon, Robin Straub, Janet Trenchard, Philip Wagner;

Joseph Stroud's Sunday poets gathering with Paul Berner, Barbara Bloom, Robin Chace, Jenny D'Angelo, Kathleen Flowers, Angelika Frebert, Diana Hartog, Ted Kagy, Rosie King, Joanna Martin, Tom McKoy, Maggie Paul, Dee Roe, Joan Safajek, Carol See, Tilly Washburn Shaw, Debra Spencer, Lesley-Anne Taylor, Beth Vieira, Philip Wagner, Joan Zimmerman;

Amber Coverdale Sumrall's retreats at the New Camaldoli Hermitage; workshops with Ellen Bass, Dorianne Laux and Joseph Millar at Esalen; Poetry Center San Jose workshop with Nils Peterson and Sally Ashton; Poetry Santa Cruz workshops with Lola Haskins, Vijay Seshadri, Vern Rutsala and Lewis Turco, D. Nurkse, Lorna Dee Cervantes, Eva Salzman;

Hummingbird Press poets Charles Atkinson, Barbara Bloom, Angie Boissevain, Simon Hunt, Rosie King, George Lober, Joanna Martin, Maggie Paul, Kim Scheiblauer, Tilly Washburn Shaw, Debra Spencer, David Sullivan, Amber Coverdale Sumrall, Ken Weisner.

CONTENTS

Into Being

Door

Deep in a dream
I am a lone pilgrim,
walk the ancient city
arrive at a door

It opens
I enter
and find myself
in the company
of a great silence

I kneel
and fall under its spell

Waking,
I call that presence
God

and ask
How I would know
What fool would I be
to say
what God is?

What fool to say
what is not God?

May I be
fool enough

to wander
through that door

to listen again
and again
for
that silence

When I Crawled Out of the Cave

It was night, but there were
stars, the Milky Way, the moon,
and they were asking questions
when I wanted to be the one asking.
I had to admit right away
that I would be of little or no help,
that their questions were deeper than mine,
and I would like to hear their
answers.

Answers? they replied.

*Welcome. These questions
are your new home.*

First Humans

Have you ever noticed
that we see only the past,
as if walking in a forest
with our backs turned
toward that great darkness,
the future, the only thing
which can possibly keep us
honest? Do you ever feel it
peering over your shoulder?

Do you ever feel we have handed over
a great part of our minds
to those who would own us and do?

Did you ever realize that a human being
can rationalize anything, and thus
believe, and promote anything?
Do you ever ask yourself
whether there is any light
shining down on this world?

Since Jesus and so many others
taught us to love one another
and we have learned to perfect
many thousandfold the means of slaughter,
do you ever wonder how we might find some way
to renounce those means, that power?

May we even be, each one of us,
the first human? Do you ever feel
that great wonder at what we are
and that yearning
for what we still might become
in a distant future
or the next moment?

Do you ever want to look out
with the eyes of a true human
into your own still first-human eyes
with forgiveness?

Sometimes in the night
do you hear the low moan of the earth turning
and know some day you must release it
and your own body, must give it all away
with whatever tenderness you can muster?
Do you ever ask your still unknown self
to grant you the strength to live,
to give to each moment that same love,
knowing we are living, may ever be living
in brutal, ancient times?

Cave Art

It's late, I'm tired.
Soon leopards
and bearded goats
begin a long journey
across the wall,
then a lone eagle
and a salmon
heavy with milt.

Even the trees,
the long grass,
and the unmoving stones
find their voices,
and I hear them.

What are they
doing on my walls?

When I see a shaman
with a tail, horns,
and three eyes
stoop and kneel,
I can't help myself
and fall to my knees.

Here I learn
to live my life.

Yet Another Revelation

Night is an indigo flower whose throat slowly opens. I step in, then gently slide fully inside. I die but do not know I die. I am given an audience with the trees and stand in their shadows. I am allowed to ask questions, but the answers disappear softly in the shadows. I receive more flowers with their tender petals and lovely scents. I soften the soil and offer water in return. Eventually I am returned to the mouth of the flower and gently step out. I look over my gifts, bow, and thank the flower. I wonder whom I am thanking.

Who Is That Singing?

Before there were words
there was song. Have you ever noticed
what a good listener God is?
To sing, you must listen for the song.

My wife says the Philosopher's Stone
is a pebble she found in a stream as a child.
She has good ears, so she should know.

We may wonder about the beginning of time,
but at any moment we are still
the beginning of ourselves.

As a child I dropped a secret I didn't understand
wrapped around a stone into a well.
Ever since then I have been drinking from that well
and learning to listen for the song.

Another Drop

One morning you wake and walk to the river,
look down and see yourself there in the river.

Write down every question you have, then
go and place each one carefully on the river.

I need time; I need peace.
I need to be alone. I need a river.

I head to the desert, look up at night and see
the Milky Way, God's own starry river.

You can shake the blues, shake your enemies,
even your friends, but you can't shake a river.

You are the tops, but maybe that's not all.
If you need to get out of town, there's always the river.

Len, you have been and done many things.
One day you will see how you are part of the river.

Blossom

of tears
sometimes
opens first,
throat knows
before lips or tongue,
even listens
then speaks,
saying
without sound

The Trees

I walk slowly among trees
waving gently
in the breeze. Soon
I can't help it
and begin to wave
with them. They
are speaking to me
with their bodies
and I speak to them
in return. I find no words
for what either of us
is saying, but they
have been here
so much longer than I
and must know
what they're doing.

They might even be holy beings
and this wind and our waving
a kind of communion.
It stirs them and they
pass it along to us.

Can you see them?
Do you understand?
It's a kind of language.
We must have all been trees.

Conversation

I walk to the forest,
sit on the redwood duff
and meditate. When I open my eyes,
several stones are sitting
before me. One by one they
ask me their questions.

Do we have free will?
Is time a piece of eternity?
How can we transcend
the unceasing pull of desire
and attain true freedom?

All I can offer them
is my praise for the depth
of their inquiry.

They say they have all the consolation
they need, resting firmly against
God's skin. Surely
I must have learned so much more
through walking, which must be,
they say, a way of talking with God
with my feet.

Unknown Ghazal

Welcome, make yourself at home, here in the unknown.
Don't worry, you can find a way deeper into the unknown.

Seeker of knowledge? Show us the way!
Knowledge is a partially lit path into the dark unknown.

I've done a lot of math, proved a lot of proofs.
Guess what's just beyond the outer edge of the known.

Being curious means you never get bored.
You can always find a road into the unknown.

Out beyond the stars and dark matter, dark energy—
now you're really talking about the unknown.

Len has long been a serious follower since he realized
what brought us here is the blessed unknown.

The Longing

The vines of tender jasmine that cover the fence
and strangle other plants in spring
must be trimmed each year.

They are made of longing.
As are the long branches of the persimmon tree
that would break under the weight of their own fruit
if we did not trim them
because we long for persimmons.

You and I and all growing things
are made of longing. Even the stars
formed in the longest night we can imagine
from the dust left by that flash
that opened out into everything
could be called a kind of longing.

In the morning I ask myself
to not impose my own limitations
on my image of God.
In the night I ask myself
whether we are made
by and of the longing.

Family

My Aunt Daphne
lived to be almost ninety-eight
but refused to celebrate
her birthday. She didn't believe
in age. My wife is the same way.
They do have a point.

The DNA in every cell
of my body is a record of the coupling,
the union, of two living cells from my parents,
as was their DNA,
and that of all our foreparents.
So I am to some degree also
all of them and share their birthdays,
all the way back to the time
when the planet was a child
and cells began replicating.

So I am four billion years old
and related to every living being
on our planet.

And now the papaya and grapes
I have just eaten and the almond milk
I have drunk are from kin.
I was brought up Catholic,
but now everything I eat
is a sacrament, is a god sacrificed
that I might live this near-eternity
in some sense forgiven.

Each day I wake surrounded by family,
take a deep breath,
and thank the billions of cells in my body.
And I thank family
as I now thank you
for each loving thing you do
for our family.

Black Spots

This morning there are four workmen
on the roof, sounding like thunder,
tearing off the old shingles
and tossing them into the dump truck
in the driveway.

They tell us there is dry rot,
which we knew already
from a few black spots
near the peak of the living room ceiling.

We are grateful.
Without these workers,
and countless others,
we'd still be living
in a cave
or would never have lived at all.

So I take my miracles
as they come,
even those black spots
on the ceiling
who just dropped in one day
to tell us something.

Into Being

The child was born
without eyes or ears or tongue,
without knowing.
The doctor stroked
the first breath in,
and the infant released
its cry for life
as the mother gasped,
the father threw his hands
toward God, then over his face.

After the tears,
the doctor spoke:

I can only speak from my own
incompleteness
and offer the words I find:

Each day, each hour you can,
touch the bare lids and whisper,
Here, the flaming sun
and here, the weeping moon.

Touch on each side the ears
that open the shield of the skull,
Here, the tender song
of the mourning dove.

Touch the hollow
where there are teeth
but no tongue,
Here, your own voice.

And you must listen
as you never have before.
Each cry,
even the deepest silence
is speaking.

Why?

The Basic Question

Review by Sarah Bakewell of Jim Holt's *Why Does the World Exist?*, *New York Times Sunday Book Review*, August 2, 2012

1.

There is a wisdom
in the taking up of difficult,
even impossible questions,
for we are reminded
that we are ever fools
and thirsty.

2.

I am an avid admirer
of questions. Rumi tells us,
Only God. I strive
to answer my prayers
as best I can.
Every photon of light
sent out by a star
and not absorbed on its way
to the distant curved reaches
eventually swings back—
there is only so much,
even of nothing,
but there's no end to it all.
Sometimes I take to chanting
quantum field equations,
for apart from being a tool
of educated prophecy,
their chief value is the power
to take us deeper
into mystery. A day
without beauty and
pain is not complete.
Aren't they two wings
of the same bird?

The greatest strength
of any theory
or any other
kind of question
is to bring us to our knees.

3.

God is to be forgiven
the rending of eternity
into lowly time. Each day,
each gasp of air only deepens the tear,
yet is a brushing up against
the airless breath of eternity. This
is the cross on which Christ
hung and on which we dangle
and flail in our dance
with arms lifted
as a plane groans by,
neighbors bounce a basketball,
and a single leaf
of the Mexican orange tree
shuddering in the wind
starts to fall.

4.

This flaw in everything—not
even nothing is perfect—we hear
so clearly from
the microwave chime
out beyond the stars
everywhere ringing
in perfect pitch an eternal
afterscream of the instant
of universal birth.

This helps me understand better
my own failings
of which I am also reminded
from several directions
with a certain frequency
such that now I invite
them to be my teachers,
to walk with me
in the neighborhood.
And before bed,
instead of prayer,
I bless one of my
weaknesses for all the help
it offers me and ask it
to guide me through the night
and the following day.

                    5.
I was too big at birth
and my mother torn—blessing
comes from blood and yields
yet more. This Jesus knew
accepting the crown and cross,
sacrifice makes holy
what is offered, we
are a gift offered. I count
my gifts, a fool, knowing
I know not
what I am counting,
this blessing, drink deep
this stain, this blood
of the gods.

6.

We don't know what this world
is, for it is never enough
and filled with infinite longing,
arms thrown open wide, bursting
into song that has no end.

We may foolishly call this
the Creation, the Big Bang
or just Nature,
yet we don't know what
we're talking about. The difference
between the worship of God
and astrophysics is really one
of musical notation, something
at which we are quite clumsy
because we hear
only part of the song.

Don't despair, just listen
as attentively as you can
and when you can't help it,
burst into song,
write down what you can
in whatever notation you have
and pass it on. You
are part of the song.

The Forest

Time is a way of sneaking in and out
of eternity. In every house
there should be a room without clocks,
a room like a forest,
where you can be alone
with everything in the world.

When there are too many clocks,
the world has a way
of ending. The end of the world
means it's time to check the fuse box
and maybe unplug a clock or two.

To walk on our hind legs
requires a certain degree
of balance
learned over the course
of millions of years.

Passing in and out
of eternity asks even more.
Any man who burns another
at the stake
has yet to open Christ's invitation
to join him in heaven.

Sometimes I dress up
in my heart and other times
in my head. I'm not fool enough
to go around pretending to wear
my soul. I am grateful
when without my knowing
it asks me to step ever so gently
into the forest.

The Haunting

When I was young and camped overnight
there were voices.
Were they deer, coyote, mountain lion, bear,
or leaves in the wind?
I could never tell.

I found the road to the hills
haunted, too. And the way home.

For decades I tried to understand
the quantum field,
that measure of probability, of possibility,
but like everyone, I failed.
Uncertainty
is a kind of haunting.

And the dark energy, too,
that flings the stars, the galaxies
away from each other,
deeper into the night.

And that little mystery
of why there is anything at all.

I do not go to the hills
for their peace or their beauty.
I go
for their haunting.

The Fashioning of Wings

requires such delicate care
just ask any bird
she'll never tell
the secret even you know
of the fashioning of wings
there is no such thing

surely by now you see
you'll never be free
of the fashioning of wings
for there is no such thing

each day I grow older
I can't even speak
how much I adore
the fashioning of wings
grateful there is no such thing

A Little Mystery

Inside each thing
is the possibility
of everything

Don't worry
we'll never find it all

Even these stones
and mud we call Earth
are a child of the Heavens
with a touch of Hell

They help hold us here
for this fleeting
eternity

which is another word for time
another word
for gazing out the window
a bit

Sometimes in the morning
you even remember
that dream
you slept all the way through

but did you ever dream
our little mystery
would be
like this?

The Elephant Trunk Nebula IC 1396

photo by Rolf Geissinger
brings me to my knees.
Perhaps we have a humble God
we can but indirectly glimpse
through this scene.

Absence
can be a kind of presence.
The greater the absence,
the more
it is always with us.

God Only Knows

I could
try to believe
what I was told about God,
but God
might not
agree with me.

I could
follow great teacher
after teacher
after teacher,
but God
still might not
agree with me.

I could fall
into despair after despair
that there is no God,
but God
just might not
agree with me.

At times I long for God.
Even deeply.
But now
I no longer need
anyone,
not even God,
to agree with me.

Error

What good is a day without error, without a wound.
Praise the error, thank the teacher, kiss the wound.

Look, I'm a scientist. All we can prove is error.
We seek an ever-finer knife of data to cut a deeper wound.

Between heaven and earth is planted a cross.
The opening thus made is both path and wound.

Praise incompleteness, it's what we're made of.
Praise the journey, follow the river of wounds.

I sure don't know what God might be,
but I love to lift song, fall in ecstasy into that wound.

Len knows there's something wrong with each thing he says.
He digs on and thanks the Unknown for every wound.

Solid Ground

I could never get the hang
of walking on water.
Each time I tried,
I received a revelation
that I was all wet.

Now I stay on solid ground,
take my daily walk
on a tectonic plate
residing in a crust
that rests on an upper mantle
over a lower mantle
floating on a molten core
which surrounds a solid core of mostly iron and nickel,
at least according to
the Preliminary Reference Earth Model
to which I am a recent convert.

Then I return to my lovely home
which was under construction
during the last major earthquake.

I hereby make a solemn vow
to remain ever on solid ground.

Praise Our Reach

The soul is so deep
that the bucket
we lower into the well
never finds it.
This is why we thirst.

God is so high
that the song
which rises
in our throats
cannot reach
what it longs
to be.
This is why we sing.

Science and Mysticism

walk into a bar,
bare their teeth, snarl,
and decide to have it all out
in the back alley,
each accusing the other
of not knowing what
he's talking about.

They circle for the longest time,
until they shout together,
Oh no! We're both right!
The unknown never goes away,
we only drive it deeper,
it's really our friend—
without it
we'd both be out of a job.

So let's drink!
More mystery!
And they drink deep.

Search Party for God

The earliest shamanic cave paintings are forty thousand years old,
and each new generation is still the first to know everything.

I gotta admire the design of church spires:
they point in every direction, but never at me.

Each blink of the eyes is a not-knowing.
Each breath a cry of longing.

I have read a lot of books, am still trying to understand stuff,
and by my next lifetime will forget it all. That must be why I
    write.

While you're at it, encourage your children to ask questions.
And your children's children should encourage theirs, too.

We are all in this party, even atheists. Agnostic Len is comforted
when he considers that God may be in the party, and searching,
    too.

The Witch Doctor Will See You Now

a brief history of human thought from prehistory to modern
science

First the nurse warns me:
You must understand
that he can only help you
if he has the same illness,
is also infected with
this wanting to know
universal truths.
But you may be in luck—
I can hear him singing now.
You may go in.

He is also dancing
and then stops to ask me,
How long have you had this problem?
He has kind eyes.
I ask, *Was there a time*
before eternity?

Now he sings again,
and soon we are both dancing,
yet not singing the same song.
Then it takes forever,
but before we know it,
we agree on one thing
and together sing:
It's always only
our best understanding,
best understanding,
always only...

Reminders

Whole worlds come into being
and after billions of years explode into dust
never seen.
This world is made by humble gods.

The wound
by which we enter this world
is made by longing.

Your spine
is what connects your tail
to your brain.

The true birthday present
is being present
to this mystery of birth and death.

Listen.
The silhouettes on the wall
have voices.

The most important things to write
are those impossible to write.

Here, take this key.
It opens invisible doors.

The Way Home

By My 135th Lifetime

I began to wonder whether eternity is really all it's cracked up to be. I just had to find out, so my wife and I, we got ourselves a dirigible. At first, we had seven clocks and calendars to help the time along, but they were always fighting, so we tossed them overboard and tried to really live in eternity, which is kinda like time except hopefully you never get tired of it. Somehow along the way we discovered a stillness, a little taste for eternity, which managed to mellow us, for a while anyway, until the helium ran out and we landed right here, somewhere on the outskirts of nowhere. We have now lived a considerable time in our little well-grounded dirigible and continue to indulge in our little eternity together whenever we find the time.

A Simple Bow

After a few days at Lake Dal in Kashmir, my friend CP and I head into the Himalayan foothills, taking a day's hike on a barely discernable path across the snow. The air is cold, the sky clear. I have never seen so much sky. We don't talk a lot. Even in India, you can only say Wow! so many times. But we are walking in sky.

Along the way we come upon a young Indian man and woman bringing firewood to their hut from hills carved nearly bare by humans seeking a little warmth. The couple confer briefly and invite us in for tea. The man motions for us to bend low so as to not breathe the smoke, then to sit on the floor by the fire beneath the rough hole carved in the ceiling. They prepare and serve the tea, conversing in Hindi with my friend, a graduate student almost fluent, while I understand little. We warm our feet, our bodies, and slake our thirst on their delicious tea. I wonder what it's like to live here—here in the sky.

Finally when we stand up to leave and thank them for their welcome, we are amazed at our fortune, both halting a few seconds searching for words. I feel something that came over me once while observing the night sky—that even in our day there is a great night between the stars and a silence deep within us, and they make a kind of home that welcomes us, is even the original welcome.

In this tiny dwelling as we part, I feel that sky. No Namaste is spoken as we each make a simple bow and I think silently—
I bow to the sky within you.

20 Aphorisms

Every flower is a book on love and survival.

Shipwreck goes over better on the second date.

There is no declarative without a capital "I."

Daily my gods are humbled.

Philosophy is the process of following the longings of the mind.

Belief and Unbelief are two forms of the failure to sustain longing.

A canticle a day keeps the metaphysician away.

History tells us: When you are sated from dining on the gods, you can take up eating the world.

Authority, that poor substitute for morality. Morality, that poor substitute for love.

For every psychological problem there's a metaphysical solution.

Not only is all one, it's much more than that.

There might be another world, or even many, but we hardly even know this one.

What do I believe in? Scratching my head and paying attention.

On a sphere, every point is the top and the bottom.

God has many forms, and one of them is nonexistence.

If hanging out by an abyss is not your thing, take up knitting.

Eternity is the opening of an eye. Each moment a veil.

I stay away from superstitions—they bring bad luck.

A human being can rationalize anything.

The easiest person for me to fool is he with whom I have the most practice.

The Empty Church

That's what the sign says out front,
but it's not always empty. No services,
sermons, or choir, still people come
to play the organ and sing
because the acoustics are great
and it's not big. Everything
and everyone is heard.

The woman who owns it
saw it come on the market
and grabbed it up
when the price stopped falling,
using her inheritance.

She took out most of the pews,
leaving just a row against each wall.
Friends come with their coffee
and chat. Homeless sleep
and move on. Mostly it's quiet.

She says she doesn't know
if there's a God, but at least here
no one gets in the way.

For some, the quiet is enough.
Just to be in the presence
of the unknown
is about as holy as it gets.

It Is Possible

that by fashioning God
after ourselves
we do not fully
apprehend God

and by using data
from scientific instruments
we cannot fully
apprehend God

and by using
the full range of human capabilities
we cannot fully
apprehend God

and that once in a while
we do not fully apprehend
ourselves
and our own foolishness.

Choosing the Pope

is hard.
Making history.
After all, at times
he holds himself to be
infallible,
and who knows where
that might lead?

But then, we are all
making history,
whether scanning headlines
during breakfast,
then heading out the door,
or raising children.
It is hard.

And we all at times
feel that swelling of
the infallible.

So I try to remember
that choosing the pope
and making history
is hard
and can be hard
on us.

Rescue

Perhaps we are all rescues,
but Ken and Coco surely are.
With twenty-eight years in recovery,
for them, rescue is daily,
their survival, work, and joy.
So the same day their vet called to say
a Bernese Mountain Dog-Airedale Terrier mix
would be put down,
they put on their work shoes,
headed to the shelter
and brought home Kylie.

Coco is a master trainer
of dogs. But some things,
such as love,
cannot be trained,
arise from nature, are given
and returned. And so it was
one evening eight years ago
when Coco was away
on a weekend retreat for women
and Ken lay on his back in bed
deep in a stroke, unable to move
or wake, his stomach emptying
from his mouth over his chin, neck,
and blocking his nose.
We never know
what a dog is thinking, but
Kylie climbed onto the bed
and sat on Ken's chest,
forcing air out, clearing
the nose,
then he licked
the face and neck clean
and Ken could breathe again.

The Hawk on Halterman Avenue

waits, perched on a ten-foot pole
at the edge of the yard
on the street corner.

Below, a five-year-old boy
wants something to happen
while his mother cautions him
to respect the bird,
stay a distance.
I watch from across the street.

Yesterday a woman brought a dead mouse for feed.
He waited until she left the fenced yard,
swooped and brought it back to his perch.
Today nothing.

Perhaps a yearling,
he must learn to make his own way.
I return in an hour;
high atop the power pole, he watches.

Today I walk, my eyes
scan the tops of poles.
He has moved on.

I remember how at age thirty-three
I finally left the university,
knowing I still had so much to learn.
Now at seventy I say,
We learn and then we die.

Drop

I am a drop of water
have journeyed thousands of miles
in rivers and oceans
risen into the sky
and fallen thousands of feet

I have nourished trees
animals, humans, worms

I am also called Love, yes
I am called Love

May I Have This Dance?

May I be held in your sway
and you in mine
for this one and only moment
we call now.
Or may we dare to spread rumors
that it lingers forever
even since that time before time
had even begun.

After all,
eternity begins again
each moment,
showing us how to dance,
to step, holding your hand
and more,
never knowing what we hold
and yet daring to dance.

Flashes in the Night

I am chased by a tiger and fall, land on the carpet,
    softening the blow.

I am living again on Spargur Drive, where I grew up.

I attend the same church in Granada, sit in the same pew
    with Federico Garcia Lorca.

With poet friends I buy some land in which the words
    of William Everson have been embedded. This helps us write.

A Moslem man develops a driverless car which uses Zip
    codes. Then a driverless rocket. He finds the Zip code for
    heaven and takes off.

A man looks up and tells me to look, that he can see the sky
    falling.

I work for Trader Joe's, advise them on what cars and dogs
    they should sell.

A poet friend has some extra names available and gives me
    one: Thunder Squiggle.

I dance a Flamenco Buleria solo onstage.

Waking

It looks like
I still have the same
wife and house, so probably
still have the same name.
I guess time is still working
and doing its job
on me, and taking its time.

The crows in the persimmon tree
are acting up as usual—
what a relief.
So, once again,
it looks like I have not
just been reborn.
But I'd better get up
and check a bit more,
just to make sure.

Just Another Dharma

As I wake this morning, what makes me think that this is the same universe I was in the day before? Is it that seemingly familiar shade of yellow coming from the east through the blinds? Is it the clock which seems to know what time it is and thus there must be something called time? Is it my wife's soft breathing? I don't know, but you can't fool me. Not this time. This time the universe really did spring into being just now and this is the one fresh and fleeting moment of existence. Just look at that ever-changing shade of light. I can't believe it. In the light there's a hint of orange-purple I've never seen before. This shade has no name. Look while you have the chance. Now. This is it. This is forever. And forever may not last very long.

Duty

The first duty of the poet
is to be
dumbstruck.

The second
is to articulate
some thread
of the delicate beauty
of that state.

The third
is to fashion it into
a transmissible
infection.

Growing Up

I was so lucky
to grow up on Spargur Drive
with apricot trees,
good neighbors,
friends my age,
and so lucky that day
I was maybe eight years old,
playing catcher
when Gail Navarro
stepped up to bat
and swung so wildly
she hit me in the head,
so lucky to have a skull
more solid
than my judgment
about where to place my head.

And now, sixty-four years later,
I'm still so lucky
as I take on so much
that sometimes I can't handle it all,
forcing me to ask myself
if I couldn't just learn a bit more, please,
about choosing where to place my head.

I Take Notes

because the fence
with its weight of vines
and blackberries
shrouds us
from the world
and the world from us
and is mostly invisible

because the sky
now wearing
its favorite blue cloak
with a few white clouds
gathered here and there
is mostly invisible

because you and I
and the angels and God
are mostly invisible

that is why
I take notes

because
even the few notes I take
are mostly invisible

because all of this
is scary miraculous

because I must

Dear Mystery

who created
the first moment
and thus every other

who poured yourself
in plenty
into that moment

challenging
our brave and pitiful
want to know so much

I honor you
by swallowing my own
pitiful want
drop by drop
in this long
and infinitely short
life I live

bathing

each moment
in the unknowable
you

A Blessing

At four and half billion years old,
our solar system has another five billion or so
before the sun cools down
to a mere eight thousand degrees,
becoming a Red Giant,
and expands to share this heat with us.

So we just might have time
to think things over a bit, be grateful,
and each do our part
to make things good here for now.

Meanwhile, a blackbird has landed on the table
and preens his shimmering feathers.

Today

I take a morning walk,
pick up a fallen leaf
and tell it my troubling
waking dream.
The leaf tells me
we must be grateful,
for this world is spinning
so we can live
more than a single day
or single night,
live and dream,
live and be born
to a new life
again and again.
I thank the leaf
and continue
my morning walk,
holding the fallen leaf.

Blue Sky

for now
but shading
toward white
in the west
with the sun
sinking toward the bay,
once again
taking its light
behind this giant
yet infinitesimal earth
so it can
hide from us
just a little while

meanwhile we will again
long to see all of the invisible
even though it is plentiful
every night
with our wildest telescopes
grabbing every photon
they can for us
in the darkest night
as we learn so much more
yet know so little

and our hunger grows
only deeper

In My 395th Lifetime

We aimed to live
at least
until we died.
We understood that
language was beyond us
and we were beyond
language. Each breath
turned to song,
each song strengthened
the breaths that followed.
We strove to render
each moment
as a work of art
and make our art
release the future.
Our longing filled us,
sustained us, for as long
as we could breathe.

The Goddess

is not all-powerful,
nor seeks to be.

The goddess
does not claim
infallibility,
nor crave it.

Sometimes
you can feel
the goddess
in the room,
the field,
the river,

sometimes
deep
in the ocean,
the stars.

Giving

The beginning of time
gave so much
and I still wonder
where this lovely rolling earth,
and even time and space,
came from.

The sun lifts water into the sky
until the clouds get so heavy they
shade and cool the lakes and oceans
until the rain falls,
which clears the sky
so the sun shows
its muscle again.

Even death is like that—
making room so others
can be born,
fresh to learn
and grow muscles, sinews and bones
so we can make anew.

I don't know how I could
possibly be thankful enough,
but I work at it.

The Way Home

Let us suppose
just for a moment,
as I do once in a while,
that God is everything,
including the unknown,
which is much greater
than the known,
and let us suppose
that each thing
is a tiny part of God
and God is still
deep in the process
of creation,
will always be
giving birth,
growing up
and learning,
living and dying,
which is why,
at times,
things may appear
a bit rough.

And we humans
are such tiny fragments
of God,
stumbling along,
living and dying,
learning our way,
and this is why,
at times,
we may appear
foolish.

And let us keep in mind that
time
is the process of eternity,

learning
is the process of knowing,

and being lost
is part of the way home.

Len Anderson is the author of two previous collections of poems, *Invented by the Night* (Hummingbird Press, 2011) and *Affection for the Unknowable* (Hummingbird Press, 2003), and a chapbook, *BEEP: A Version of the History of the Personal Computer Rendered in Free Verse in the Manner of Howl by Allen Ginsberg,* now on the internet at http://www.bestmindsofmygeneration.com/. He was born and raised on the San Francisco peninsula and received his BA and PhD in physics from UC Berkeley. He worked in experimental elementary particle physics at Berkeley and École Polytechnique in France. In private industry he developed sensors for the automation of paper manufacturing for 16 years and retired in 1997. His poetry has appeared in journals including *Caesura, Catamaran Literary Reader, DMQ Review, DNA, Hilltromper, Miramar, The Montserrat Review, Porter Gulch Review, Phren-Z, Rattle, Red Wheelbarrow, The Sand Hill Review, Sparring with Beatnik Ghosts* and the anthologies *Quarry West: Poets and Writers of the Monterey Bay, The Anthology of Monterey Bay Poets 2004, Harvest from the Emerald Orchard,* and *Crow and Raven Anthology.* He has received a nomination for a Pushcart Prize and is a winner of the Dragonfly Press Poetry Competition and the Mary Lönnberg Smith Poetry Award. He is a co-founder of Poetry Santa Cruz and serves as Secretary-Treasurer. He and his wife live in the Live Oak area in Santa Cruz County.